CELEBRITY SECRETS

FILM STARS

LIZ GOGERLY

PowerKiDS
press
New York

Published in 2012 by The Rosen Publishing Group, Inc.
29 East 21st Street, New York, NY 10010

First Edition

Senior Editor: Camilla Lloyd
Designer: Stephen Prosser

Picture Acknowledgments: The author and publisher would like to thank the following for allowing their pictures to be reproduced in this publication:Cover and 9: Stewart Cook/Rex Features; © Armando Gallo/Retna Ltd./Corbis: 8, 14, 22 (middle); © Sara De Boer/Retna Ltd./Corbis: 22 (top); Kevin Mazur/WireImage/Getty Images: 15; 20th Century Fox/Everett/Rex Features: 1 and 19; Alex J.Berliner/BEI/Rex Features: 5; Screen Gems/Everett/Rex Features: 7; David Fisher/Rex Features: 10; Fox Searchlight/Everett/Rex Features: 11; Walt Disney/Everett/Rex Features: 13; Buena Vista/Everett/Rex Features: 17; Charles Sykes/Rex Features: 20; A©RIA Novosti/Topfoto: 21; lev radin/Shutterstock: 2 and 6; Entertainment Press/Shutterstock: 4, 18, 22 (bottom); Cinemafestival/Shutterstock: 12,16, 23(middle and bottom); Brandon_Parry/Shutterstock: 23 (top); Jim Barber/Shutterstock: 24.

Library of Congress Cataloging-in-Publication Data

Gogerly, Liz.
 Film stars / by Liz Gogerly. — 1st ed.
     p. cm. — (Celebrity secrets)
 Includes index.
 ISBN 978-1-4488-7037-0 (library binding) — ISBN 978-1-4488-7084-4 (pbk.)
 — ISBN 978-1-4488-7085-1 (6-pack)
 1. Motion picture actors and actresses—Biography—Juvenile literature. I. Title.
 PN1998.2.G64 2012
 791.4302'80922—dc23
 [B]

                                                    2011029065

Manufactured in Malaysia

CPSIA Compliance Information: Batch #WW2102PK: For Further Information contact Rosen Publishing, New York, New York at 1-800-237-9932

Contents

Zac Efron

HIGH-SCHOOL HERO

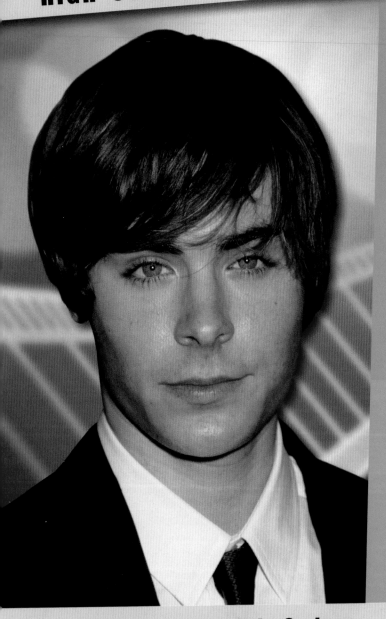

Zac attends the annual Palm Springs Film Festival in 2009.

Zac was offered a record deal by music impressario Simon Cowell, but turned it down because he wants to be taken seriously as an actor.

Stats!

Name: Zachary David Alexander Efron

Date of birth: October 18, 1987

First hit movie: Playing Troy Bolton in *High School Musical* in 2006.

Films: Zac kicked off his film career in 2003 in *Melinda's World*. He starred in *Miracle Run* (2004) and *The Derby Stallion* (2005) before *High School Musical* was released in 2006. He sang and danced his way through *Hairspray* (2007), *High School Musical 2* (2007), and *High School Musical 3: Senior Year* (2008). After *High School Musical* he was in *17 Again* (2009), *Me and Orson Welles* (2009), and *Charlie St. Cloud* (2010).

Career highlights: Up until now it's been working on *High School Musical*. Zac talks about making the film as a kind of adventure that changed his life. He also values the friendships he made with his fellow cast members. "We've grown up together. It's been a real high school experience," he has said.

Personal life: Zac began dating actress Vanessa Hudgens when they filmed the first *High School Musical*. The young lovebirds are such an item that they are now known as "Zanessa!"

Secrets of success: It's those sparkly blue eyes, dazzling smile, and a floppy mop of hair. He really can sing, dance, and act, too!

Life Story

Right now Zac Efron is probably the biggest teen screen idol in the world. The *High School Musical* films proved he could sing and dance his way to the top. He is inspired by Johnny Depp and Leonardo DiCaprio. Now he's on a quest to show he has what it takes to be a serious dramatic actor.

Zac was born in San Luis Obispo, California and raised in the small town of Arroyo Grande, California. He has a younger brother, Dylan, and two dogs. Zac had a normal middle-class childhood and by the age of 11 he showed signs of having a talent for singing. Stage performances soon led to parts in television series including *Summerland* and *ER*. He graduated from high school in 2006. By that time, he was already working on the Disney blockbuster *High School Musical*. Zac had the grades to get into college, but he took a shot at acting instead. He claims that getting the part of Troy Bolton was pure luck. The musical *Hairspray* sealed his reputation as an entertainer. Now Zac is seeking even more interesting roles.

Zac and Vanessa at the *Charlie St. Cloud* premiere in July 2010.

Questions and Answers

Q   Which actor do you look up to?

A   *"One person comes to mind for me, Leo [DiCaprio]. I think Leo is a guy that's been through all this. I'm sure he knows how this felt. He persevered and stuck to his guns. He made cool movies and some that didn't work so well. He's doing it and he's survived, and, just now, he's started to make some of the coolest movies of his career."*

Zac Efron, collider.com, July 2010

Q   What do you want to do next in your career?

A   *"I just want to make great films and be good in them. And I think that my perception of what's great in a film is constantly evolving. It's growing up, so I'll want to try different things. But I'm not going to do anything for the sake of changing my image. It's just not that important to me. I think that will come with time. I think you earn respect."*

Zac Efron, The Guardian, November 2009

Amanda Seyfried

MAMMA MIA!

Amanda at the premiere of *Letters to Juliet* at the Tribeca Film Festival in April 2010.

Amanda's close friends call her Nana because she loves to knit.

Stats!

Name: Amanda Michelle Seyfried

Date of birth: December 3, 1985

First hit movie: Amanda's first lead role was in the hit movie *Mamma Mia!* in 2008. She starred alongside huge stars such as Meryl Streep, Pierce Brosnan, Julie Walters, and Colin Firth.

Films: Amanda's first movie was *Mean Girls* in 2004. Early films include *Nine Lives* (2005) and *American Gun* (2005). After *Mamma Mia!* she played lead parts in *Boogie Woogie* (2009), *Jennifer's Body* (2009), *Dear John* (2010), *Chloe* (2010), and *Letters to Juliet* (2010). In 2011 she starred in *Red Riding Hood*, a film produced by Leonardo DiCaprio.

Career highlights: So far it has to be *Mamma Mia!*. She says: "It changed my life — careerwise, lifewise, lovewise."

Personal life: Amanda has dated some of her co-stars. She fell for actor Dominic Cooper on the set of *Mamma Mia!*. He lived in London, England, so work commitments often kept them apart. She says she has no plans to marry until she's 35 or 40.

Secrets of success: Lots of young, ambitious actresses are beautiful with long blonde hair. With those green eyes, though, Amanda has something more. She shines in front of the camera. She's also down-to-earth and tries to keep away from the whole celebrity scene.

Life Story

Amanda Seyfried is suddenly a big box-office hit. *Mean Girls* and *Mamma Mia!* got her noticed and lead parts in *Dear John* and *Letters to Juliet* mean she's a star.

Amanda was born in Allentown, Pennsylvania. She has an older sister named Jennifer. Amanda became obsessed with acting after watching the 1996 film *Romeo + Juliet*.

Amanda claims that film is the reason why she

Questions and Answers

Q How easy was it to play the part of Sophie in Mamma Mia!?

A *"It was pretty simple for me to just be excited, and that's the character I play. She's just enthusiastic about life, and I was so enthusiastic about filming that I didn't really have to go any place to get the right attitude. It was a very rare experience — Greece and Meryl and Pierce (Brosnan) and dancing and singing…"*

Amanda Seyfried, Philadelphia Daily News, *July 2008*

Q How do you stay so grounded?

A *"Maybe people [in Hollywood] wear really nice clothes, and they drive really nice cars — but that doesn't make me comfortable. And if I'm not comfortable, it won't be a part of my life. There's something empty about having your own VIP booth, and people staring at you, drinking and dancing…"*

Amanda Seyfried, Glamour, *April 2010*

Amanda in *Dear John* with Channing Tatum.

became an actress. When she was 9 she began acting classes and she was soon signed with a modeling agency. She modeled until she was 17, but the dream of becoming an actress was always there. Through high school she took acting classes and studied opera. Later she starred in *Grease* and *A Christmas Carol* and got her first television acting jobs. In 2004 she made her film debut in *Mean Girls*.

Ten years after first watching Claire Danes and Leonardo DiCaprio in *Romeo + Juliet*, she got her first big break on television. Amanda was a lead character in the family drama *Big Love* from 2006 through 2010. *Big Love* meant Amanda was known in the United States, but it was her part in *Mamma Mia!* that brought her recognition around the world.

Robert Pattinson

VAMPIRE AND HEARTTHROB

Robert on a photo shoot for
The Twilight Saga: New Moon.

Robert has played the guitar and piano since he was a kid. He wrote and performed two songs for the first *Twilight* movie.

Stats!

Name: Robert Thomas Pattinson

Date of birth: May 13, 1986

First hit movie: Robert was an overnight sensation when he played vampire Edward Cullen in *Twilight* (2008).

Films: *Harry Potter and the Goblet of Fire* (2005), *How to Be* (2008), *Twilight* (2008), *Little Ashes* (2009), *The Twilight Saga: New Moon* (2009), *Remember Me* (2010), *The Twilight Saga: Eclipse* (2010), *Bel Ami* (2011).

Career highlights: Robert had to beat 3,000 other hopefuls to get the part of Edward Cullen in the movie *Twilight*. Playing the good-looking vampire has brought him fame and fortune, but Robert insists that playing Salvador Dali in *Little Ashes* was the turning point in his career. It was the first film where he had to give serious thought to the character.

Personal life: Robert says that girls never used to like him until he played the sultry vampire. Now he gets so much attention he's scared to go out! It is rumored that he's dating his *Twilight* co-star Kristen Stewart.

Secrets of success: Girls go crazy for his messed-up hair and sculpted cheekbones. Behind the looks is a serious and intelligent actor.

Life Story

The *Twilight* films are a worldwide sensation. These days Robert can hardly leave the house without hordes of fans or paparazzi following him. It takes a team of 25 bodyguards to protect him during filming.

Robert was born in London, England, and is close to his parents and two older sisters. It was his father who encouraged him to join Barnes Theatre Company when he was 15. At 17 he got his first real acting part in the film *Vanity Fair* with Reese Witherspoon. His scenes were edited out, but the following year he played Cedric Diggory in *Harry Potter and the Goblet of Fire* (2005).

After that, Robert did some work in the theater and he took a few small parts on television. He even tried having a music career.

Robert and Kristen attend the premiere of *The Twilight Saga: Eclipse* in June 2010.

Stephenie Meyer, the author of the *Twilight* books, described vampire Edward Cullen as "the most beautiful creature who has ever been born." Modest and shy, Robert never expected to win the part. He did not expect the films to become so popular either.

The *Twilight* films have kept him very busy, but he's managed to work on other projects, too. Lead roles in the films *Little Ashes* (2009) and *Remember Me* (2010) show there is more to Robert than being a beautiful vampire.

Questions and Answers

Q Do you enjoy being a teen idol?

A *"I have been lucky, of course. Last year, if I went out, I'd have to fight to chat someone up. This year, I look exactly the same, which is really scruffy, and yet lots of people seem to have just changed their minds and decided I'm really sexy."*

Robert Pattinson, The Telegraph, March 2010

Q What do you think of your sudden fame?

A *"They [his parents] think it's more impressive than I think it is. It's just luck for me. It's totally random. I never set out to achieve anything—not like fame or anything. It's strange. But there are things I want to do with it. I still have to learn how to make my life work."*

Robert Pattinson, The Scotsman, November 2009

Carey Mulligan

THE BRIGHT STAR

Carey Mulligan with her BAFTA, 2010.

Carey loves to ski. These days she has to be more careful because she fears an accident could harm her acting career.

Stats!

Name: Carey Hannah Mulligan

Date of birth: May 28, 1985

First hit movie: Carey's first film was *Pride and Prejudice* with Keira Knightly. Carey played Kitty Bennett, the younger sister of Elizabeth Bennett.

Films: *Pride and Prejudice* (2005), *When Did You Last See Your Father?* (2007), *Public Enemies* (2009), *An Education* (2009), *Brothers* (2009), *The Greatest* (2010), *Wall Street: Money Never Sleeps* (2010), *Never Let Me Go* (2010).

Career highlights: At just 24 years old, Carey earned critical acclaim and plenty of awards for her portrayal of Jenny Miller in *An Education*. She cherishes her Best Actress award from the British Academy of Film and Television Arts (BAFTA) and was amazed to be nominated for an Oscar in 2010.

Personal life: Carey first kissed a boy when she was 16 and she was 19 when she had her first real boyfriend. She began seeing her *Wall Street: Money Never Sleeps* co-star Shia LaBeouf in 2009, but they broke up in 2010.

Secrets of success: Carey is a natural-born actress. She hasn't been to acting school but she's wanted to act since she was 6 years old. Critics admire her versatility. They claim she could be the next Audrey Hepburn.

Life Story

Carey Mulligan is like a breath of fresh air. She's young and down-to-earth and she took the film world by storm in *An Education*. Now the young English actress with the cropped hair and unique style is in demand.

Carey was born in London, England. She was 3 years old when her father took a job managing hotels and the family moved to Germany. For the next eight years the family lived in hotels. Carey's love of acting first started when she watched her big brother perform in the school play *The King and I*. She began to cry because she wanted to be in the play, too. Eventually she was given a small part and went on from there to star in more school plays.

Questions and Answers

Q What does it feel like to be compared with the film icon Audrey Hepburn?

A *"It's flattering, but a little freaky. She's, like, a goddess. She didn't have Shrek cheeks and a wonky mouth."*
Carey Mulligan, The Mirror, February 2010

Q Did you always dream of being an actress?

A *"I used to have these dreams when I was 14 in which I would be working with Judi Dench. Then I would wake up and realize it wasn't real. So when I got the part in* Pride and Prejudice *with Judi Dench and told my parents, they didn't believe me."*
Carey Mulligan, USA Today, February 2010

Carey's parents tried to persuade her to go to college but Carey secretly applied to drama school instead. Even though she was rejected Carey still wanted to act. She then decided to write to actor and screenwriter Julian Fellowes. He introduced her to a casting agent and in 2004 Carey made her debut in *Pride and Prejudice*. She appeared in a string of television dramas before starring in the theater production of *The Seagull*. Carey was a hit in London and on Broadway in New York.

Since *An Education* Carey has been snapped up to play parts in big Hollywood movies such as *Wall Street: Money Never Sleeps*. Carey claims she isn't looking to become a big leading lady. She's says she's looking for interesting roles. One thing is for sure—many people are interested in seeing what Carey does next.

Carey with Keira Knightley in *Never Let Me Go* in 2010.

Jake Gyllenhaal

THE PRINCE OF PERSIA

Jake at the Cannes Film Festival in 2009.

Jake is a fitness fanatic whose boyhood dream was to play soccer for the United States in the World Cup.

Stats!

Name: Jacob Benjamin Gyllenhaal

Date of birth: December 19, 1980

First hit movie: *October Sky* (1999)

Films: Jake's first film was *City Slickers* (1991) when he was 11. Other top performances include: *Donnie Darko* (2001), *Bubble Boy* (2001), *The Good Girl* (2002), *Moonlight Mile* (2002), *The Day After Tomorrow* (2004), *Brokeback Mountain* (2005), *Jarhead* (2005), *Proof* (2005), *Rendition* (2007), *Brothers* (2009), *Prince of Persia: The Sands of Time* (2010), *Nailed* (2010).

Career highlights: Jake became a household name when he played Jack Twist in *Brokeback Mountain* (2005). The romantic movie caused a stir because Jake plays a ranch hand who falls in love with another man played by Heath Ledger. Jake was nominated for an Oscar for Best Supporting Actor for his part.

Personal life: Jake has dated actresses Kirsten Dunst, Natalie Portman, and Reese Witherspoon. The death of his friend Heath Ledger was a terrible blow in 2008.

Secrets of success: Jake isn't afraid to try out different roles. He's played the romantic lead, the war hero, and more recently an action hero in the film *Prince of Persia: The Sands of Time*.

Life Story

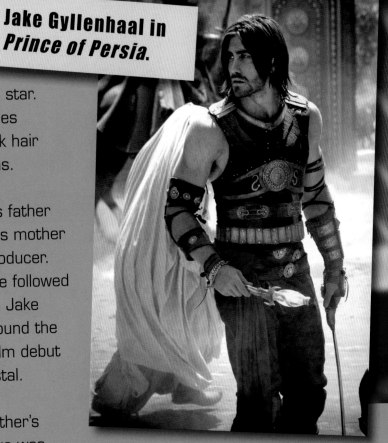

Jake Gyllenhaal looks every bit the movie star. Muscular and standing at 6 feet 2 inches (1.9 m) tall, he fills the screen. Yet his dark hair and piercing blue eyes hint at hidden depths.

Jake was born into a filmmaking family. His father Stephen Gyllenhaal is a film director and his mother Naomi Foner is a screenwriter and film producer. Both Jake and his older sister Maggie have followed their parents into the industry. As children Jake and Maggie performed their own plays around the house. When Jake was 11 he made his film debut in *City Slickers* playing the son of Billy Crystal.

Jake made appearances in some of his father's films, but his parents were protective. Jake was allowed to audition for other parts as long as he didn't accept any offers of work. They also made sure that Jake did part-time summer jobs such as waiting on tables or working as a lifeguard.

After high school Jake went to Columbia University to study philosophy and Eastern religions. He dropped out after two years to concentrate on acting. Jake made a name for himself in the cult indie film *Donnie Darko* (2001). He proved his versatility as an actor in 2005 playing a ranch hand in *Brokeback Mountain*, a marine in *Jarhead*, and a mathematical genius in *Proof*. Jake will tackle any movie role, great or small. He thinks he'll complete his degree one day, too.

Questions and Answers

Q What is it like to star in a film like *Prince of Persia*?

A *"Working on a movie like Prince of Persia was awesome. It was great fun to be an action hero and to jump around, running off walls and fighting and having great quippy lines. And wearing only half of your clothes, of course!"*

Jake Gyllenhaal, The Telegraph, January 2010

Q What do you think of your fans?

A *"I pride myself on making interesting films, as opposed to the type that just draws a huge audience of teenagers, so I think they are pretty smart fans. They always have questions for me, something that hasn't been answered by the movie. They'll scream: 'What's the ending of Donnie Darko? I don't understand it!' That is so nice."*

Jake Gyllenhaal, Daily Mail, 2007

Kristen Stewart

FEISTY LEADING LADY

Kristen at the photo shoot for *The Twilight Saga: Eclipse* in 2010.

Kristen likes to spend her free time with her three dogs, Oz, Jack and Lily. She also has a cat called Jella.

Stats!

Name: Kristen Jaymes Stewart

Date of birth: April 9, 1990

First hit movie: Kristen's first lead role was in the 2002 film *Panic Room*, playing the daughter of Jodie Foster.

Films: *The Cake Eaters* (2007), *Into the Wild* (2007), *Twilight* (2008), *Adventureland* (2009), *The Twilight Saga: New Moon* (2009), *The Yellow Handkerchief* (2010), *The Runaways* (2010), *The Twilight Saga: Eclipse* (2010).

Career highlights: Kristen shot to stardom playing feisty heroine Bella Swan in the *Twilight* films. Her performance has won many awards including MTV awards for Best Female Performance and Best Kiss (shared with Robert Pattinson).

Personal life: Kristen began dating actor Michael Angarano when she was 14. The pair met while filming the television movie *Speak* (2004). Ever since the *Twilight* sagas hit the big screen people have wondered if she is going out with Robert Pattinson. Kristen and Robert's on-screen chemistry is so strong fans think they must really be in love!

Secrets of success: Kristen likes to truly believe in her characters so she can give them depth. This allows her to give really honest performances.

Life Story

Kristen Stewart never set out to be a Hollywood star. The success of the *Twilight* films was something she never expected. Playing Bella Swan has turned her into one of the most famous actresses in the world.

Kristen was born in Los Angeles, California. Kristen's family are all involved in the film industry behind the scenes. Her father is a stage manager and producer while her mother, Jules, is a script supervisor. Kristen was eight when she opted for a career in front of the cameras. She got her break when a talent scout saw her in a school play. After a few minor roles she finally landed the part in *Panic Room*. Kristen was a good choice because she looked like Jodie Foster, who played her mother. Kristen impressed the critics.

Questions and Answers

Q What do you think of the first *Twilight* movie?

A *"I'm really proud of Twilight. I think it's a good movie. It was hard to do, and I think it turned out pretty good. But I don't take much credit for it. So when you show up at these places, and there's literally like a thousand girls and they're all screaming your name, you're like, why? You don't feel like you deserve it."*

Kristen Stewart, USA Today, February 2009

Q What have been the downsides of playing Bella?

A *"What people told me [when I signed on to Twilight] was that there would be a lot of fan girls, people who love the books. But people don't tell you that as long as you're living in Los Angeles, it's a show every second of your day. It's like the Kristen show. And it's so boring!"*

Kristen Stewart, Allure Magazine, October 2009

Kristen's sensitive portrayal of the trailer-park teenager in *Into the Wild* (2007) grabbed people's attention. She was working on the indie film *Adventureland* (2009) when she heard she'd won the part of Bella Swan. Kristen went on to play Bella in the next two *Twilight* films. She also played rock star Joan Jett in the *The Runaways* (2010). Being Bella has had its downsides, though. Kristen is mobbed by fans constantly and rarely goes out. She remains level-headed and believes the *Twilight* phenomenon will fade. Meanwhile, critics think this young star is about to shine.

Kristen and Robert win an award for the best screen kiss at the MTV Awards in 2010!

Johnny Depp

THE PEOPLE'S FAVORITE

Johnny at the Venice Film Festival in 2009.

Johnny plays the guitar. He's made guest appearances on albums by Oasis and Shane MacGowan (of the Pogues). He's also a member of the band P.

Stats!

Name: Johnny Christopher Depp II

Date of birth: June 9, 1963

First hit movie: *Edward Scissorhands* (1990) was Johnny's first serious dramatic role. He was nominated for a Golden Globe Award for Best Actor.

Films: Johnny's film debut was in the horror flick *A Nightmare on Elm Street* (1984). His classic movies include: *Cry Baby* (1990), *What's Eating Gilbert Grape?* (1993), *Don Juan DeMarco* (1995), *Donnie Brasco* (1997), and *Sleepy Hollow* (1999). In 2003 he starred in the first of four *Pirates of the Caribbean* films. He also starred in *Finding Neverland* (2004), *Charlie and the Chocolate Factory* (2005), *Sweeney Todd* (2007), and *Alice in Wonderland* (2010).

Career highlights: Johnny admits that his favorite part is playing Captain Jack Sparrow in *Pirates of the Caribbean*.

Personal life: Johnny was briefly married in his early twenties. He later dated actress Winona Ryder and model Kate Moss. These days he enjoys a long relationship with French actress Vanessa Paradis. They have two children named Lily-Rose and Jack.

Secrets of success: Johnny follows his instincts and often plays eccentric characters. This keeps his fans hooked!

Life Story

Johnny Depp has played many strange characters. His portrayal of pirate Captain Jack Sparrow earned him an Oscar nomination. In *Charlie and the Chocolate Factory* he played a peculiar Willy Wonka and was nominated for a Golden Globe. He's yet to win a big award, but the fans adore him and the critics applaud him.

Johnny Depp has homes in Los Angeles, France, England, and even owns a private island in the Bahamas. He's a doting father and a caring partner to girlfriend Vanessa Paradis. Home and family matter a great deal to Johnny, probably because of his own troubled childhood. He remembers bitter fights between his parents. The family also moved more than 30 times. He was 15 when his parents finally divorced. Shortly afterward he dropped out of school and began playing in bands. He was in a band called The Kids when he moved to Los Angeles.

First came a lead part in the film *A Nightmare on Elm Street*. Then, Johnny's lead role in the series *21 Jump Street* made him a teenage heartthrob. Once again it was Johnny's good looks that got him noticed. By now Johnny was tired of being labeled a teen idol. Instead he took a risk and played the lead in Tim Burton's *Edward Scissorhands*. This time it was Johnny's performance that got him noticed. He was nominated for a Golden Globe Award for Best Actor. Ever since, Johnny's career has been all about taking risks. He must be doing something right because in 2010 Johnny won the People's Choice Award for Actor of the Decade.

Questions and Answers

Q **What's with that rebel attitude of yours?**

A *"My youth? Who's to tell. I don't like conventions. Like to set my own rules. I never choose a great Hollywood production. I want to play in movies that tell something. Movies about people, about emotions as emotions really are."*

Johnny Depp, Avantgarde, September 2009

Q **What is your recipe for success?**

A *"Just luck really. I've just been very lucky over the years. You know it's a miracle that people still hire me after some of the stuff I've gotten away with! So, I lay it all down to luck!"*

Johnny Depp, DevonandCornwallfilm.co.uk, May 2010

Zoe Saldana

ALL-OUT ACTION GIRL

Zoe at the Independent Spirit Awards in California.

Stats!

Name: Zoe Yadira Zaldana Nazario

Date of birth: June 19, 1978

First hit movie: Zoe first caught our eye in *Pirates of the Caribbean: The Curse of the Black Pearl* (2003). Zoe played Anamaria, the fiery female pirate who puts Captain Jack Sparrow in his place with a slap.

Films: *Center Stage* (2000), *The Terminal* (2004), *Haven* (2004), *Guess Who* (2005), *Star Trek* (2009), *Avatar* (2009), *The Losers* (2010), *Death at a Funeral* (2010).

Career Highlights: Zoe says that playing Neytiri in *Avatar* was her most challenging role to date. Nobody actually saw her face in the James Cameron epic, but now everyone knows her name!

Personal life: Zoe has been with her boyfriend Keith Britton for over ten years. The couple met when he was working as a model and she was starting out as an actress.

Secrets of success: Zoe has brains and beauty. She looks athletic and enjoys playing strong female characters.

Zoe's grandmother and great-grandmother were seamstresses. Now, the actress has launched her own fashion line called Arasmaci.

Life Story

In the summer of 2010 at Milan Fashion Week, Zoe Saldana was chosen as "The Face of the Future." She was selected for her talent, grace, and beauty. Zoe has all these things, but she loves nothing better than being a strong leading lady.

Zoe was born in New Jersey to a Puerto Rican mother and Dominican father. The family moved to Queens, New York, when she was a baby. When she was nine years old her father died in a car accident. Zoe's mother struggled to raise Zoe and her two sisters. They lived in the Dominican Republic for a few years. Zoe studied ballet at the ECOS Espacio de Danza Dance Academy, a leading dance school on the island. She also discovered a passion for science fiction movies. Sarah Connor from *The Terminator* and Ripley from *Aliens* were big role models.

Zoe moved back to New York when she was 17. There she joined a theater group and discovered her talent for acting. In 2000 she made her film debut in *Center Stage*, a film that called upon her dancing and acting skills. These days Zoe is happy to play the action heroine. In 2009 she played a steely Lieutenant Uhura in the new film version of *Star Trek*. As Neytiri, the Na'vi princess in *Avatar* she got to do most of the stunts herself. In 2010 Zoe played another feisty female in the film adaption of the comic book *Losers*. Zoe is fast becoming known for playing it tough. Fine comic performances in *Guess Who* (2005) and *Death at a Funeral* (2010) suggest Zoe has a bright future.

Questions and Answers

Q Who inspires you?

A *"He [James Cameron] was why I got into movies. His female heroes—Ripley from Aliens and Sarah Connor from The Terminator—showed me that an actress can be an action hero."*

Zoe Saldana, flixster.com, March 2010

Q Do you think of yourself as Dominican or American?

A *"I don't understand labels. I don't need anybody to tell me I'm Latina or black or anything else. I've played characters that were written for Caucasian females, I just want to be given the same consideration as everybody else, and so far that has been happening."*

Zoe Saldana, flixster.com, March 2010

Zoe in *Avatar*.

Daniel Radcliffe

OUR FAVORITE WIZARD

Daniel at the Tony Awards in 2010

Daniel has never learned to ride a bike or swim. He has a mild form of dyspraxia, a neurological disorder which means he finds coordination difficult.

Stats!

Name: Daniel Jacob Radcliffe

Date of birth: July 23, 1989

First hit movie: *Harry Potter and the Sorcerer's Stone* (2001).

Films: *Harry Potter* films: *Chamber of Secrets* (2002), *Prisoner of Azkaban* (2004), *Goblet of Fire* (2005), *Order of the Phoenix* (2007), *Half-Blood Prince* (2009), *Deathly Hallows: Part I* (2010), *Deathly Hallows: Part II* (2011). In 2007 he decided to take a small role in the Australian film *December Boys*.

Career highlights: Daniel cried when he heard he had won the part of Harry Potter for the film adaptation of J. K. Rowling's famous book. He says being chosen to play Harry was one of the most defining moments of his life.

Personal life: In *Harry Potter and the Order of the Phoenix* we saw Harry's first screen kiss. In real life Daniel was looking for a girlfriend. In 2009 he began dating Laura O'Toole, his co-star from the theater production of *Equus*.

Secrets of success: Despite fame, fortune, and frequent flights of fantasy on a broomstick, Daniel manages to keep his feet on the ground. As of 2010 he was one of the richest teenagers in the world. He likes to spend his money on CDs and books and still takes his laundry home for his mother to wash!

Life Story

Harry Potter is one of the world's most well-loved characters. Daniel has grown up being Harry. At the same time the world has watched Daniel grow as an actor and mature into a young man.

Daniel was born and raised in London, England. Actors and literature have always been part of his life. His father was a literary agent and his mother was a casting agent. The family regularly went to the theater. At the age of five Daniel knew he wanted to be an actor. His television break came in 1999 when he played young David in the BBC production of Charles Dickens' novel *David Copperfield*. In 2001 he made his film debut in *The Tailor of Panama*. By then he had already been chosen to play Harry. Thousands of young hopefuls had auditioned for the part of a lifetime. When Daniel was chosen, author J. K. Rowling said there couldn't be a better Harry! Cameras began rolling on the first film, *Harry Potter and the Sorcerer's Stone*, in October 2000. The final scenes of the last installment, *Harry Potter and the Deathly Hallows: Part II*, were filmed in June 2010. In the early days Daniel had to juggle schoolwork with his acting career. He left school in 2006 and admits he learned more on film sets.

Now Daniel is looking for new acting experiences. In 2007 he caused a stir when he appeared naked in the theater production of *Equus*. His biggest role since *Harry Potter* has been in the film *The Woman in Black*. Critics are eager to see if there's more to Daniel than being Harry Potter.

Daniel and Emma Watson in *Harry Potter and the Half-Blood Prince*.

Questions and Answers

Q **Do you worry that people will forever see you as a schoolboy wizard?**

A *"A lot of people will be generous and open-minded enough to see me as other people. But I think that to a lot of people I will always be Harry."*

Daniel Radcliffe, TimeOut London, 2009

Q **What will you do next?**

A *"I want to keep acting. I want to test myself. For now I just want to try things and see. I would love to work in America. I wouldn't love to live there, but I'd love to experience working there."*

Daniel Radcliffe, TimeOut London, 2009

OTHER FILM STARS

Michael Cera

Career

Background: Michael wanted to become an actor when he saw Bill Murray in *Ghostbusters*. He was only four at the time but soon got involved in weekend acting classes. He auditioned for hundreds of commercials and television programs before being picked for a part in the Canadian kids program *I Was A 6th Grade Alien* when he was 11.

Films: *Superbad* (2007), *Juno* (2007), *Youth in Revolt* (2010), *Scott Pilgrim Vs. the World* (2010).

Career highs: From 2003–2006 he played awkward teenager George Michael Bluth in the popular television comedy *Arrested Development*. The series was cult viewing and for those in the know Cera was a star in the making.

Favorite Actors: Bill Murray, David Cross.

Hobbies: Playing the guitar, tennis.

Web site: www.michaelcerasource.net

Basic Information
Home: Born in Brampton, Ontario, Canada. Lives in Brampton and Los Angeles.
Birthday: June 7, 1988

Freida Pinto

Career

Background: Freida performed in a few plays while she studied English at a university in Mumbai but nothing professional. After college she modeled for two years and starred in a few television commercials. She presented the travel show *Full Circle* before taking a three-month acting workshop.

Films: *Slumdog Millionaire* (2008), *You Will Meet a Tall Dark Stranger* (2010).

Career highs: Even though she had no professional acting experience, film director Danny Boyle wanted Freida to play his leading lady in *Slumdog Millionaire*. Freida was nominated for many awards.

Favorite Actors: Jack Nicholson, Johnny Depp, Marilyn Monroe, and Nicole Kidman.

Hobbies: Dancing and theater.

Basic Information
Home: Born in Mumbai, India. Lives in Malad, Mumbai.
Birthday: October 18, 1984

Will Smith

Career

Background: Will first hit the scene in the 1980s as a rap star performing with Jeff Townes as DJ Jazzy Jeff and the Fresh Prince. From 1990 to 1996 he starred in the popular television comedy *The Fresh Prince of Bel-Air*. *Independence Day*, *Men in Black*, and *I Am Legend* have all proved huge box-office draws, making him one of the most successful Hollywood actors today.

Films: *Six Degrees of Separation* (1993), *Independence Day* (1996), *Men in Black* (1997), *Ali* (2001), *Men in Black II* (2002), *I, Robot* (2004), *Hitch* (2005), *The Pursuit of Happyness* (2006), *I am Legend* (2007), *Hancock* (2008).

Career highs: Will says that playing boxer Muhammad Ali was the peak of his career. He was tested physically, emotionally, and spiritually by the part. He was rewarded with an Oscar nomination for Best Actor.

Favorite Actors: Eddie Murphy, Richard Pryor, Tom Hanks.

Hobbies: Producing films, rapping, fencing, and watching basketball.

Web site: www.willsmith.com

Basic Information
Home: Born in Philadelphia, Pennsylvania. Lives in Miami Beach, Florida.
Birthday: September 25, 1968

Taylor Lautner

Career

Background: Taylor was ten years old when he told his parents he wanted to become an actor. From the age of six Taylor had been learning karate. It was his karate teacher who told him to try acting. In 2003 the Lautner family moved to Los Angeles so Taylor could follow his dream of becoming an actor. A few television and bit parts in movies followed. Taylor was 13 when he got his big break, playing the lead role in *The Adventures of Sharkboy and Lavagirl in 3-D* (2005).

Films: *Cheaper by the Dozen 2* (2005), *Twilight* (2008), *The Twilight Saga: New Moon* (2009), *The Twilight Saga: Eclipse* (2010), *Valentine's Day* (2010).

Career highs: Taylor is one of Hollywood's hottest young stars, thanks to playing Jacob in the *Twilight* films. He loved getting the chance to beef up and play the action scenes in *New Moon* and *Eclipse*.

Favorite Actors: Tom Cruise, Mike Myers, Jessica Simpson.

Hobbies: Karate, football, baseball, dancing to hip-hop, screenwriting, and directing.

Web site: www.taylorlautner.org

Basic Information

Home: Born in Grand Rapids, Michigan. Lives in Los Angeles, California.

Birthday: February 11, 1992

Angelina Jolie

Career

Background: Angelina is the daughter of actors Jon Voight and Marcheline Bertrand. Her parents split up when she was a baby. She made her screen debut at the age of seven in *Lookin' to Get Out*. At 11 she attended the Lee Strasberg Theatre and Film Institute. After dropping out of school she tried modeling but returned to acting at 16. Her first major role was in *Hackers* (1995). It was the lead role in *Lara Croft: Tomb Raider* (2001) that turned her into an international star.

Films: *Cyborg 2* (1993), *George Wallace* (1997), *Playing By Heart* (1998), *Pushing Tin* (1998), *The Bone Collector* (1999), *Lara Croft Tomb Raider: The Cradle of Life* (2003), *Mr. & Mrs. Smith* (2005), *A Mighty Heart* (2007), *Wanted* (2008), *The Changeling* (2008), *Salt* (2010).

Career highs: Angelina won a Golden Globe for her portrayal of supermodel Gia Carangi in *Gia* (1998). In 1999 she won an Oscar for Best Supporting Actress for *Girl, Interrupted*.

Favorite Actor: Brad Pitt.

Hobbies: Flying (she has a pilot's license for a single-engine aircraft), humanitarian work.

Basic Information

Home: Born in Los Angeles, California. Has homes in Los Angeles, New Orleans, New York, France, and Italy.

Birthday: June 4, 1975

Russell Crowe

Career

Background: Russell Crowe spent a lot of his childhood in Australia. He got his taste for acting on the movie sets where his parents did the catering. His first acting job was in a theater production of *The Rocky Horror Picture Show*. After starring in Australian movies, he made his Hollywood debut in *The Quick and the Dead* (1995). His career picked up after a critically-acclaimed performance in the 1997 gangster flick *L.A. Confidential*.

Films: *Romper Stomper* (1992), *The Insider* (1999), *Gladiator* (2000), *A Beautiful Mind* (2001), *Master and Commander: The Far Side of the World* (2003), *Cinderella Man* (2005), *3:10 to Yuma* (2007), *Robin Hood* (2010).

Career highs: Russell won the Oscar for Best Actor for his powerful performance in the historical epic *Gladiator*.

Favorite Actors: Marlon Brando, Jodie Foster, Nicole Kidman.

Hobbies: Horseback riding, riding motorcycles, performing with his band 30 Odd Foot of Grunts.

Basic Information

Home: Born in Wellington, New Zealand. Lives in Sydney and Nana Glen, New South Wales, Australia.

Birthday: April 7, 1964

Glossary

ambitious (am-BIH-shus) The desire to do well.

audition (ah-DIH-shun) A test of the abilities of a performer.

career (kuh-REER) A job.

debut (DAY-byoo) A first public appearance, as of a performer.

director (dih-REK-ter) The person who tells movie or play actors what to do.

recognition (reh-kig-NIH-shun) Favorable notice or attention.

role (ROHL) A part played by a person in a movie, TV show, or play.

talent (TA-lent) A natural ability or skill.

versatility (ver-suh-TIH-luh-tee) The ability to do many different things well.

Index

Web Sites

Due to the changing nature of Internet links, PowerKids Press has developed an online list of Web sites related to the subject of this book. This site is updated regularly. Please use this link to access the list:
www.powerkidslinks.com/celeb/film/